THIS JOURNAL BELONGS TO

____